Book Design: Sandra Bottros

ST SHENOUDA PRESS
8419 Putty Rd,
Putty, NSW, 2330
Sydney, Australia

www.stshenoudapress.com

ISBN: 978-0-6488658-3-4

I0080916

"Who are you?" she shouted.

It was dark and we were all asleep except for our mother. I woke up at her voice but could not see who she was talking to.

"Noufri, the Lord wants one of your children to serve Him," I heard someone telling her.

Suddenly I could see a very bright light shining from a person dressed in white... it was an angel speaking with our mother!

She seemed very afraid but obediently answered, "They are all here to serve the Lord!"

To my surprise, the angel pointed to Bishoy, my youngest brother!

1

"The Lord chooses Bishoy, your youngest son," he said to her.

She tried to convince the angel to choose me or one of her other five sons, since Bishoy was the youngest and the weakest of us.

However, the angel spoke again and said, "The Lord's power will be revealed in Bishoy, despite his young age. This is the one the Lord has chosen to serve Him and to be a light to all people."

Our mother smiled and nodded to the angel, and as the years passed, I would always remember what I heard the angel say to her concerning my younger brother Bishoy.

When my brother, Bishoy, was just 20 years old, he left us and went to join a monastery in the desert. It was difficult for us to watch him leave, but by doing so he taught us a lesson, that serving God is the most important thing. He went there to become a monk and dedicate his life to prayer. Bishoy's teacher was a great saint called St Bimwa, who helped him to deepen his love for Jesus.

At the monastery, my brother became good friends with a monk named Fr John the Short, who was named so for being short in height. One day, Fr John was

given a dry stick by St Bimwa, who was his spiritual father too, and said,

"John my son, plant it in the ground and water it every day."

Even though it was impossible for a dry stick to grow and become a living tree,

Fr John still obeyed his father's instructions. He would walk for over an hour to

the river to collect water and then return to water the stick. After three years

of doing this daily, the stick miraculously began to grow leaves, branches and even

fruit! This became a lesson for all the monks regarding the blessings of obedience.

Later in Bishoy's life, an angel appeared to him and told him that the Lord wanted him to live alone in a nearby cave, so that he could devote all his time to prayer and fasting. So Bishoy did just that and went to the cave, which still exists today at St Mary's Monastery (El-Surian).

Bishoy would spend many hours each day reading and studying the Bible, just like we did at home when he was younger. I recall him telling us one time he visited us,

"My beloved family, if it wasn't for all the times we read the Bible together when

I was a child, I would not be so in love with it now."

His favourite book of the Bible was Jeremiah the Prophet in the Old Testament. Whenever he struggled to understand what he was reading, he would pray that Jesus opens his eyes to the meaning. Jeremiah himself appeared to Bishoy to explain the book!

He would also spend the entire night in prayer to our Lord, until the sun came up the next morning. In fact, he would tie his hair to the ceiling with a rope to prevent him from falling asleep while praying through the night.

Everyone who met Bishoy felt the peace and love that shined from him, and so he was loved by everyone. He soon had 2000 disciples who also became monks! He became known as Anba Bishoy, as he was the spiritual father for all of them. Under his guidance, the monks lived happily in the caves around the mountain, praying and fasting together every day.

This was the fulfilment of what the Lord promised Anba Bishoy. He once appeared to him and said, "Beloved Bishoy, this mountain shall be filled with thousands of blessed monks under your leadership." The monks would gather around him much like bees would surround honey,

to hear his sweet teachings about Jesus. When I heard this about him
from the other monks, I remembered how he was always an example to
his friends at school, teaching them to love God with all their heart.
Even at home he would always gather the family together for prayer
each night, although he was the youngest one.

He continued to grow in grace as he was fulfilling the command, "Till
we all come to the ... fullness of Christ" (Eph 4:13). He even attracted
the poor and needy because of his great generosity to them. Soon Anba
Bishoy became known as "the Beloved of Christ".

Living in the mountain and spending his time with God, Anba Bishoy did not care at all about money or any other riches, for he was rich with God's love. One day, a rich person brought to him a large amount of gold and silver. God had told Anba Bishoy that this would happen, and that this would be a trick from the devil. He therefore knowing that these riches would keep him away from worshipping God, refused to even look at the coins when the man brought them.

He told the rich man to take his gold and silver and give it to the

poor instead. The rich man was shocked that Anba Bishoy would refuse all this wealth. After much discussion, the rich man agreed with him, and went away to give the gold and silver coins to the poor.

Once the rich man left, Anba Bishoy went back to his cave and found the devil there frustrated and saying, "Bishoy! You always ruin my tricks with your humility!" Anba Bishoy replied, "God supports His children against your tricks! I choose to follow the Lord, who is much more valuable than any gold or silver coins."

Anba Bishoy was a loving spiritual father to the monks that lived in the caves around him. When one of his disciples sinned, he would continue praying for him until that disciple repented. He would pray for them every day so that they would stay faithful to God, and that they would grow in their spiritual lives. One time when two monks were walking past Anba Bishoy's cave, they heard a second voice inside. Knowing that he lives in the cave alone, this was very strange! As the monks got closer to the cave, they heard the following words, "Do not worry beloved Bishoy. I will always be with you. I have witnessed your

hard work and your constant love for Me. I will grant that whoever prays, asking for your intercession, will have their prayers answered."

It was the Lord Jesus present with him inside the cave!

Anba Bishoy replied, "My beloved Lord Jesus Christ, You suffered for me and for the whole world. You were crucified, died and resurrected for our salvation. I am the one that needs to thank you for listening to me and my prayers." The monks were in amazement over hearing that Anba Bishoy was in the presence of the Lord.

After knowing that Jesus appeared to Anba Bishoy, the other monks also wanted to see Him. They asked Anba Bishoy to pray so that He may ask Jesus to bless them with an appearance. They begged him, "Please ask the Lord to appear to us. We also want to see Him!"

Anba Bishoy told the disciples that he would ask the Lord for them. Later that day he entered his cave and prayed, "Lord, thank you for your love. Your sons the monks desire to see You. Please show them Yourself and rejoice their hearts." Immediately, the Lord promised to come at a specific time at the top

of the mountain, just for the monks. The monks were so excited when Anba Bishoy told them!

When the day finally came, the monks hurried to get to the top of the mountain to see the Lord. As they were running up, they passed an old sick man on the way who also wanted to come along to see Jesus. "Sorry, we don't have time to help you right now. We need to see Jesus," the monks said as they quickly ran past him. So they all ignored the old man and continued running, hoping to see Christ.

Anba Bishoy, however, saw this old man, lifted him upon his shoulders and began to carry him up the mountain. Strangely, the man began to get heavier and Anba Bishoy could not continue any further. As he stopped to catch his breath, he looked at the man's feet and was in awe ... there were 2 holes in his feet! It was the Lord Jesus Himself he was carrying! Anba Bishoy turned to Jesus saying, "My Lord, how can a sinner like me carry you, the Creator of Heaven and Earth?"

The Lord then gently spoke, "You have stopped to carry Me, dear Bishoy, while

the others were too busy to help Me. Since you have carried Me, your body will remain intact after your death, and will never decay."

When the monks didn't find Jesus at the top of the mountain, they were very upset. Anba Bishoy explained to them, "the old man you ran past was Jesus Himself. Remember what it says in Matthew 25:35, 'for I was hungry and you gave Me food ... I was a stranger and you took Me in.' Jesus is found in every weak or sick person that needs help." The monks repented and glorified God for this lesson.

There was another occasion in which Anba Bishoy saw a man who came from a long journey and was very tired from walking. So he asked him to stop by his cave, had the man rest, took off his sandals and began to wash his feet. Even though Anba Bishoy was a spiritual father to thousands of monks, he still had the love and humility to wash the feet of a stranger!

As Anba Bishoy was washing the stranger's feet, he heard a familiar voice saying, "My chosen Bishoy, you are a faithful servant!" The man then disappeared. Anba Bishoy knew immediately that this very man was the Lord

again! He recognised Him, and felt the peace and comfort in His voice. Anba Bishoy offered the water in which he washed Jesus' feet to the other monks to drink from so as to receive the blessing.

Throughout Anba Bishoy's life, the Lord continued to reveal Himself to him and to physically speak to him, because of his great love for Him. As Anba Bishoy continued to grow in spirituality and in his love for the Lord, he attracted many more followers all the way to the desert to worship Jesus, and to devote their lives to Him as monks also.

Anba Bishoy was not only a very blessed man, but a great teacher too! There was once a monk living in a town called Epsi, in Upper Egypt. This man began to preach wrong teachings about the Holy Trinity, not teaching that God is Father, Son and Holy Spirit. This was causing many problems in the Church and so Jesus told Anba Bishoy to go to the city and correct the teaching.

So, he made some three-handled baskets and took them with him. The monk who was spreading the incorrect teaching, along with hundreds of others, welcomed Anba Bishoy. Several of them noticed the three handled baskets and were curious

about them as they had never seen anything like them. Anba Bishoy explained to them that the basket was an example of the Holy Trinity being One God. Just like it is just one basket, yet three handles so there is only One God, yet Father, Son and Holy Spirit. The monks were amazed at his words and shouted, "Oh yes Anba Bishoy, the Father, the Son and the Holy Spirit are one God!"

They begged him to teach them more about the Holy Trinity, and so Anba Bishoy shared verses from the Bible with them explaining further.

It was on July 15, in the year 407 AD, that our Saviour took Anba Bishoy's soul. Years later, his pure body was carried in a large coffin to a monastery which they named after him. It was a day full of joy and celebration. The number of monks living in the desert had grown, so they decided to build a large monastery there in honour of him.

When the monks at Anba Bishoy Monastery (at a place called Wadi El-Natroun) uncovered his body years after he had died, it looked exactly the same as when

he was alive. The Pope and the monks were amazed and wondered how it did not decay! This was just as our Lord Christ had promised him when he carried Him on his shoulders up the mountain.

Many miracles have been performed from his body and by his prayers. Looking back, I never imagined that my younger brother Bishoy would become a saint. I now understand that regardless of age or size, the Lord invites His children to serve Him and become saints, like St Anba Bishoy!

THE END